Two-Minute

BIBLE STORIES

Retold by Elena Pasquali
Illustrated by Nicola Smee

All things bright and beautiful,
All creatures great and small,
All things wise and wonderful,
The Lord God made them all.

Cecil Frances Alexander (1818–95)

Contents

In the Beginning   6

Noah and the Flood   10

Moses and the Deep Water   14

Jonah and the Whale   18

Daniel and the Lions   22

Baby Jesus   26

The Lost Sheep   30

The Good Samaritan   34

Jairus and His Daughter   38

The Two Builders   42

In the Beginning

In the dark and shapeless
nothing, God spoke.

Light

And there was the
first bright, sparkling
daytime.

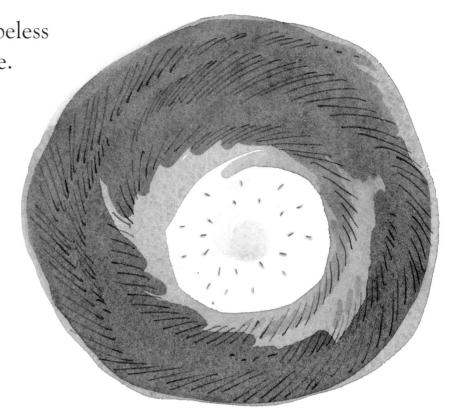

On the second day,
God spoke again.

Sky

And there was a
dome of blue above
a glittering sea.

On the third day, God's voice was quiet and low.

Earth

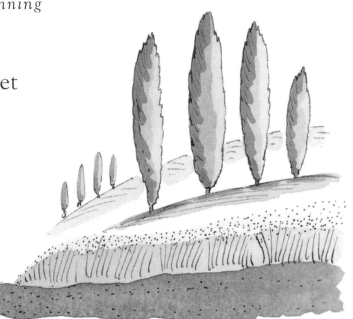

And there was good brown earth, tiny seedlings, waving corn and tall, tall trees.

On the fourth day, God called to the sky.

Shine

In the daytime, the sun shone bright and gold.

In the night-time, the moon shone silver. Tiny stars twinkled all around.

twinkle

On the fifth day, God sang:

Come alive

Fish swam in the seas and birds flew through the air.

On the sixth day, God's voice rang out again. Animals came rustling through the forests and running over the plains and leaping across the mountains.

8

In a kindly voice, God said:

Friend

The boy and the girl smiled.
'You are special to me,' said God. 'Your children will be special to me… and your grandchildren, and your great grandchildren and their children's children for ever.'

On the seventh day, God only whispered as the sun came up.

Rest

It was a day to enjoy the wonderful world.

Noah and the Flood

Long ago, on a sunny day, God came to talk to Noah.
'I'm sad about the world,' said God. 'It has all gone wrong.'

'I know,' said Noah. 'It's people. They can be so bad.'

'And so,' said God, 'I'm going to send a flood. It will end the old world. Then I will start again.'

'Oh dear,' said Noah. 'Whatever will I do?'

'You will build a boat,' replied God.

'Will I?' asked Noah.

'You will take your family on board,' said God.

'And you will take the animals on board, two of every kind.'

'How will I do that?' asked Noah.

He sounded worried.

'I'll help,' said God cheerfully.

'Then I will send the rain.'

11

And God did.

It rained and rained and rained.

The flood came up. The boat floated away.

'Is it ever going to stop raining?' asked Noah.

God did not say anything.

pitter patter
splish splish

Inside the boat, Noah tried to be cheerful.

'God hasn't forgotten us,' he announced.

But he was beginning to wonder.

Then one day…

'We're aground,' cried Noah.

bump!

12

He spoke to the dove: 'Go and look for land.
We can't stay here for ever.'
The dove flew away and the dove came back.
In its beak was a fresh green twig.
'That's good news,' said Noah. 'It means the flood is going down.'

coo

When the land was dry, at last God spoke.
'Leave the boat,' said God. 'Make the
whole world new.'
'The rainbow is my promise.
Never again will I flood the world.
I will keep it safe for ever.'

roar

13

Moses and the Deep Water

The great river of Egypt was deep.
Among the rushes was a floating basket.

quack

A baby boy

A princess of Egypt came to bathe.
She looked inside the floating basket.
  'Poor little Hebrew baby. The king of
Egypt wants to harm the Hebrew babies.
A mother is trying to save her son.
  'Well, I shall keep him safe now.
And I shall give him a name: Moses.

'But I need someone to take care of him!'
A little girl stepped out from the rushes.
The princess guessed who: baby Moses' sister.
'I know someone,' said the girl.
The princess was delighted.

My little one

The little girl brought her mother. She was,
of course, the baby's mother too.
So Moses was safe from the water.

When Moses grew up, he found out about the wicked king. He found out that the Hebrew people were the king's slaves. He found out that they were treated very badly.

When he tried to help, he got into trouble. He had to run away from Egypt.

Oof!

Moses

In the wild country, he saw a strange thing: a bush was on fire, but it wasn't burning up. As he looked, he heard a voice.

It was God. God told Moses to go to the king of Egypt. 'Tell him to let the Hebrew people go free,' said God.

Moses went and asked.
The king was angry.
But God wanted the Hebrews to go free.
Nothing went right for the king or for Egypt
till at last he changed his mind.

No, no, no

Moses led his people out of Egypt.
They reached a sea. God spoke to Moses:
'Lift up your stick.'
When Moses lifted his stick, the waters moved aside.
They left a path through the sea.
Moses and the Hebrews were safe from the water.
God had set them free.

On we go!

17

Jonah and the Whale

Jonah was a prophet. If God told him something, it was his job to pass the message on. Right now, God was telling Jonah to warn the people of Nineveh. 'Tell them to stop being bad, or I will have to punish them.'

Goodbye!

Jonah did not want to obey. He wanted to see the people of Nineveh punished. He ran down to the sea. He got on a boat bound for far, far away.

In the night, God sent a storm. The sailors were very afraid.

'It's all my fault,' wailed Jonah. 'I've disobeyed God. Throw me into the sea, and the storm will stop.'

Man overboard!

God still wanted Jonah to go to Nineveh. God sent a whale, who swallowed Jonah.

GULP

The whale spat Jonah out onto a beach.

splodge

Jonah hurried to Nineveh.

He called aloud to everyone to change their ways.

The people of Nineveh listened to all he said. 'We have been bad,' they wept. 'We must change our ways.'

The king of Nineveh was saddest of all. He gave an order.

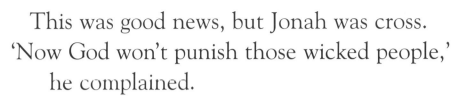

This was good news, but Jonah was cross. 'Now God won't punish those wicked people,' he complained.

Hmmph

As he sulked, a plant grew up. It gave lovely shade. In the night a worm came and ate it. Jonah was sadder than ever.

Hooray

baa

'So you care for a plant, do you? Well, I care for the people of Nineveh. And their children. And their animals.'

21

Daniel and the Lions

King Darius was in charge of a huge empire.
He needed wise people to help him.

The wisest of all was Daniel. So King Darius
gave him the most important job.

That made other people angry.

'We must get rid of him,' said one.

'I've an idea,' said another.

Well done

whisper whisper

They went to the king.

'O King, may you live for ever,' they began. 'May everyone obey you and worship you and you alone, O great and most wonderful king.'

The king was pleased.

'You must make a new law. Say that anyone who worships anyone but you will be punished. Say they will be thrown to the lions.'

The king made the law.
  The men hurried off to find Daniel.
  'There he is,' they said. 'He's saying prayers to his God. That's against the law.'

Dear God...

King Darius was most upset. He was sad to see Daniel thrown to the lions. 'The law wasn't about you,' he sobbed.

God did not want Daniel hurt. God sent an angel to stop the lions from eating him.

King Darius worried about Daniel all through the night. Then he went back to the den of lions.

Shhh
Go to sleep

roar

He called out to Daniel.
'Are you alright?'
Daniel answered. 'God has heard
all my prayers,' he said. 'God has
taken care of me.'

I'm fine

zzz

Baby Jesus

Mary's day had begun as normal. But suddenly it wasn't normal anymore. An angel had come to see her. 'God has chosen you to have a baby,' said the angel. 'God's own Son. You must call him Jesus.'

Mary was puzzled, but she agreed.

Joseph was planning to marry Mary. 'But she's having a baby, and it's not my baby,' he worried.

An angel spoke to him in a dream. 'Take care of Mary and her baby,' said the angel.

Joseph woke up and knew he must obey.

Mary and Joseph went to Bethlehem together.
  The town was crowded and there was no room.
So they took shelter in a stable.
  And there among the animals, baby Jesus was born.
  Mary laid him in a manger to sleep.

cluck

heehaw

eek

Out on the hills, shepherds were looking after their sheep.

An angel appeared.

Peace on earth

The shepherds were startled. 'Don't be afraid,' said the angel. 'I bring good news. God's Son has been born in Bethlehem. He is cradled in a manger. He will bring God's blessings to all the world.'

The shepherds went and found the baby.

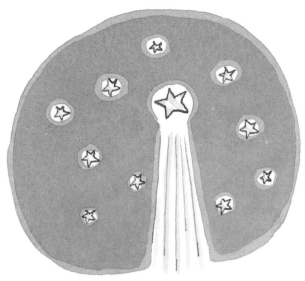

From far away came wise men. They were following a star. They were looking for a newborn king.

twinkle

The star led them to Bethlehem. They found Mary and her baby. They gave rich gifts: gifts for a special king.

myrrh *frankincense*

gold

The Lost Sheep

Jesus told this story.
'There was once a shepherd who had a flock of sheep.
   'He counted them every day.

'Then one day when he was counting, there was bad news.

One, two, three

Ninety-nine… Oh!

Take care

'One sheep was missing.

'The shepherd left the ninety-nine sheep
in the field.

'He went looking for his lost sheep.

plod

walk

'At last he found it.

baa

There you are

A party!

'The poor thing. The shepherd picked it up and carried it home.

'When it was safely with the flock, he called his friends.

'"Let's celebrate together," he said.

'"My sheep was lost, and now it's found."

'Remember this story,' said Jesus,
'and remember this too:
  'People who do wrong things feel lost and alone.
  'When they see their mistake, they are
friends with God again.
  'And all the angels celebrate.'

Tra la la

Joy!

The Good Samaritan

A man had a question for Jesus. 'What does it mean to love other people?'

Jesus told this story.

'A man was going from Jerusalem to Jericho. 'On the way, robbers attacked him. They beat him up, stole his money and left him lying in the road.

Help

Ouch

'A priest came by: it was his job to help people worship God in the great Temple in Jerusalem.

'He saw the man in the road. He walked past on the other side.

'Another man came by: it was his job to help the priest.

'He saw the man in the road. He came to look. Then he hurried on.

Oh dear

'A Samaritan came by. Samaritans don't even go to the Temple in Jerusalem.

'He saw the man.

heehaw

There there

'He went over to him.
  'He bathed his wounds.
  'He lifted him onto his donkey.
  'He led him to an inn and took care of him.

jingle

'The next day, the Samaritan had to
travel on.
  '"Here is money," he said to the
innkeeper. "Take care of that man for me.
If it costs more, I will pay next time I come."'

Jesus looked at the person who had first asked the question.
'Who showed love in that story?' he asked.
'The one who was kind,' came the answer.
Jesus smiled.

*You go and do
the same*

Jairus and His Daughter

Jairus was wiping his tears as he hurried along the street. 'She's very ill and getting worse,' he said. 'My darling daughter.'

Jairus hurried to meet Jesus.

'I've heard you can make sick people well,' he said.

'Please come and make my daughter well.'

It's horrid being ill

I hope she gets better

Jesus agreed to come.
But they could hardly move for the crowds.
And Jesus even stopped to help
someone else.

Please help me

Oh dear

Poor girl

At last Jesus and Jairus reached the house.
  Women were weeping and wailing.
  'What's the fuss about?' asked Jesus.
'She's not dead.'

He went to the room where the little girl lay.
  She was pale and cold.
  He took her hand and spoke to her.

Little girl, get up

At once she sat up. She was well again.
'She'll need something to eat,' said Jesus
to her parents.

The Two Builders

The crowds gathered round Jesus.
'Love one another,' he told them. 'Forgive one another.
'Don't worry about everyday things, but trust in God.
'If you do these things, then you are like the wise builder.
'He chose the very best place for his house.
'It was high on a rock, where the ground
was solid.

This is hard work

dig dig

'The rain came.

pitter patter

'The wind blew.

whoo

'The river flooded.

gurgle

'The house stood firm.

43

'If you do not listen to what I say, then you are like the foolish builder.

'He chose the easiest place for his house.

'It was down on the sand, where the ground was soft.

dig dig

This is easy

'The rain came.
pitter patter
'The wind blew.
whoo
'The river flooded.
gurgle

'The house fell down.
FLAT

'What a terrible fall it was!'

45